Welcome to Woodberry Way

An Inviting Collection of Delightful Quilts

Allison Jensen

Martingale
Create with Confidence

Welcome to Woodberry Way: An Inviting Collection of
Delightful Quilts
© 2021 by Allison Jensen

Martingale®
18939 120th Ave. NE, Ste. 101
Bothell, WA 98011-9511 USA
ShopMartingale.com

Printed in Hong Kong
26 25 24 23 22 21   8 7 6 5 4 3 2 1

Library of Congress Cataloging-in-Publication Data is
available upon request.

ISBN: 978-1-68356-139-2

MISSION STATEMENT

We empower makers who use fabric and yarn
to make life more enjoyable.

CREDITS

PUBLISHER AND
CHIEF VISIONARY OFFICER
Jennifer Erbe Keltner

CONTENT DIRECTOR
Karen Costello Soltys

DESIGN MANAGER
Adrienne Smitke

TECHNICAL EDITOR
Nancy Mahoney

PRODUCTION MANAGER
Regina Girard

COPY EDITOR
Sheila Chapman Ryan

COVER AND
BOOK DESIGNER
Mia Mar

ILLUSTRATOR
Sandy Loi

PHOTOGRAPHERS
Adam Albright
Brent Kane

SPECIAL THANKS
*Some of the photography for this book was taken
at the home of Libby Warnken in Ankeny, Iowa.*

DEDICATION

*To my grandmothers, great-grandmothers, and all the
creative women who came before me: Marquitta, the
cook and seamstress; Wasel, the gardener and baker;
Vela, who loved to hand quilt for her grandchildren; and
Gretta, the creative extraordinaire. I love you all so much!*

Contents

Projects

Introduction

Woodberry Way is the street where my mother grew up in London, where my grandparents lived for many decades. I grew up listening to stories of this place and was lucky enough to spend a few summers there myself. The house is tall and narrow, painted white with black trim and a red front door with colored glass. There are thoughtful details throughout—elaborate curtains sewn by my grandma and carefully considered trim work and paint colors. The stairs tuck up to the left to the second floor. My favorite room is the "green room," which overlooks the long, narrow yard, full of vibrant flowers and greenery. If you continue up the curved stairs to the third floor, you'll find a small bedroom with a slanted ceiling, floral wallpaper, exposed beams, and tall windows that show mostly sky. To me as a child, this room was pure magic. Adjacent the magical bedroom is an attic full of treasures galore. In the yard there's a curved path that leads past the trees to a playhouse where we prepared performances as children.

I never spent a winter there, other than as a baby, but the tales shared seem a part of me. By Christmas the days were damp and cold, and sundown came early due to the high latitude. After school in the winters, when my mother was riding the bus home, darkness had already come. My grandmother Marquitta (also my middle name) is a cheerful woman who seems to always sparkle. She worked to make the season festive, cooking and sewing and decorating the three-story row house for her seven daughters and one son.

In preparation for Christmas, she hid satsuma mandarins under the floorboards in a little cellar and bottles of homemade root beer in a box under the stairs. Grandma and grandpa were known to stay up all night on Christmas Eve to accomplish Christmas miracles; one year they recarpeted the entire living room overnight. Christmas Day was met with a full turkey dinner, mince and cherry pies, fancy silver goblets full of root beer, Jim Reeves on the record player, and special guests from the church and grandpa's office. The Queen's annual speech came on the TV at three o'clock, and they opened Christmas "crackers," small paper packets with trinkets inside.

Grandma could cook anything, but our favorite thing to come out of that kitchen was her chocolate pudding. My grandpa Vance had big plans and an even bigger heart. There was no project too big for him to make a reality. They both had a way of making ordinary things into an occasion, such as candles for weekday dinners.

I'd like to think that a love for aesthetics and color, finding joy in the mundane, and the excitement and courage to start a new project come from them. I hope that through these projects, you feel inspired to add color and texture to your world, and to share your creations with your loved ones. Doing so brings me so much joy!

~Alli

A Palette That Pleases

I'm a deep lover of color. A variety of harmonious colors brings me such joy! And because quilting is a year-round pursuit, I love making quilts that carry across the seasons, but that still fit in with my home's style, making those little bursts of color extra special. These are the colors that I regularly use in my home accents, and you'll find many of them incorporated into my quilts.

. . . .

Red

Red always makes me smile, and the pretty little red berries that pop out of the landscape in winter are no exception. Red is rich, bold, and joyful.

Green

The foliage that surrounds us, both indoors and out, provides fresh color and calming scents (especially at the holidays). Mother Nature mixes green with nearly everything, and so do I!

Blue

Delightful blue tones aren't hard to find any time of year. From the lightest aqua to the darkest blue sky, blue is cool and calming.

White

White isn't a true color if you're being technical, but it's an important part of nature's colorscape—icy in the winter and cool in the summer. White is clean, bright, and pure.

Gray

Gray isn't the most exciting color to see in the sky or in a quilt, but it plays an important role as a soft, moody background or a bit of darker contrast.

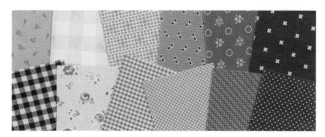

Morning Frost

Being a California girl, I had never heard the term "hoarfrost" until some of my Instagram followers mentioned it when asked what they loved about winter. When I looked it up, I understood why they would appreciate this beautiful natural phenomenon, which creates delicate swirling patterns, and I wanted to design a quilt reminiscent of its beauty. To keep this two-color, one-block quilt interesting, I picked an aqua fabric with a little sparkle and a white fabric with tiny sporadic dots. Though the pattern looks complicated, it's actually the same block throughout, just rotated to create a secondary pinwheel pattern.

FINISHED QUILT
54½" × 72½"

FINISHED BLOCK
9" × 9"

FABRICS USED

Aqua Dot on White
by Lori Holt
for Riley Blake Designs

Glimmer in Ice
by Cloud9 Fabrics

Bella Solids in Robins Egg
by Moda Fabrics

Materials

Yardage is based on 42"-wide fabric.

- 3 yards of aqua print for blocks
- 1 yard of teal solid for blocks and binding
- 2⅞ yards of white print for blocks
- 3½ yards of fabric for backing
- 61" × 79" piece of batting

Cutting

All measurements include ¼" seam allowances.

From the aqua print, cut:

4 strips, 5" × 42"; crosscut into 48 rectangles,
2¾" × 5"

24 strips, 3¼" × 42"; crosscut into 288 squares,
3¼" × 3¼"

From the teal solid, cut:

4 strips, 3¼" × 42"; crosscut into 48 squares,
3¼" × 3¼"

7 strips, 2½" × 42"

From the white print, cut:

28 strips, 3¼" × 42"; crosscut into 336 squares,
3¼" × 3¼"

Making the Blocks

Press seam allowances in the directions indicated by
the arrows.

1 Draw a diagonal line from corner to corner on
the wrong side of the white squares. Layer a
marked square on an aqua square, right sides together.
Sew ¼" from both sides of the drawn line. Cut the unit
apart on the marked line to make two half-square-
triangle units. Trim the units to measure 2¾" square,
including seam allowances. Make 576 units.

Make 576 units.

2 Repeat step 1 using the remaining marked
squares and the teal squares to make 96 units
measuring 2¾" square, including seam allowances.

Make 96 units.

3 Lay out 12 aqua half-square-triangle units, two
teal half-square-triangle units, and one aqua
rectangle in four rows. Sew the units into rows. Join
the top two rows and add the rectangle to make
the top half of the block. Join the top half and the
remaining two rows to make a block. Make 48 blocks
measuring 9½" square, including seam allowances.

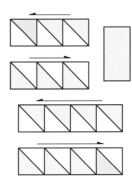 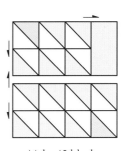

Make 48 blocks,
9½" × 9½".

Designed by ALLISON JENSEN; pieced by JANICE RAMPTON;
quilted by EMILEE HATHAWAY

Assembling the Quilt Top

Lay out the blocks in eight rows of six blocks each, rotating every other block as shown. Sew the blocks into rows. Join the rows to make a quilt top measuring 54½" × 72½".

Finishing the Quilt

For more details on any finishing steps, visit ShopMartingale.com/HowtoQuilt for free downloadable information.

1 Layer the quilt top with batting and backing; baste the layers together.

2 Quilt by hand or machine. The quilt shown is machine quilted with an allover swirl design.

3 Use the teal 2½"-wide strips to make binding and then attach the binding to the quilt.

Quilt assembly

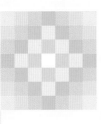

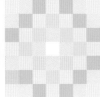

FINISHED QUILT
54½" × 69½"

FINISHED BLOCK
14" × 14"

FABRICS USED
Vintage Holiday
by Bonnie and Camille for
Moda Fabrics

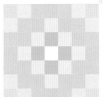

Stay-cation

Though you may only get to travel around the world in your mind, make your home a place you want to visit time and time again, like your grandmother's house when you were young. Achieve the look of a Granny Square block without having to sew on point, cut on the bias, or waste any fabric. In fact, you'll use every scrap of the precut squares with no waste. I love that!

. . . .

Materials

Yardage is based on 42"-wide fabric.

- 37 squares, 10" × 10", *OR* 37 strips, 2½" × 42", of assorted prints for blocks
- 1 yard of white tone on tone for sashing
- ⅞ yard of aqua check for border
- ⅝ yard of green print for binding
- 3½ yards of fabric for backing
- 61" × 76" piece of batting

Cutting

All measurements include ¼" seam allowances. Cut the 10" squares or 2½"-wide strips carefully; you will not have any leftover fabric. To help you stay organized, label the sets according to how many pieces are in each pile.

From *each* of 24 assorted print squares or strips, cut:
16 squares, 2½" × 2½" (384 total). Separate into *24 sets* of 12 matching squares and *24 sets* of 4 matching squares.

From *each* of 12 assorted print squares or strips, cut:
16 squares, 2½" × 2½" (192 total). Separate into *24 sets* of 8 matching squares.

From *1* print square or strip, cut:
20 squares, 1½" × 1½"

From the white tone on tone, cut:
2 strips, 14½" × 42"; crosscut into 31 rectangles, 1½" × 14½"
12 squares, 2½" × 2½"

From the aqua check, cut:
6 strips, 4½" × 42"

From the green print, cut:
7 strips, 2½" × 42"

Getting Organized

Making the blocks is easier if you take a few minutes to select the 2½" squares for each block before stitching. A white square is used in the center of each block. You'll also need one set *each* of the following (each set is a different print):

- 4 matching squares
- 8 matching squares
- 12 matching squares
- 12 matching squares
- 8 matching squares
- 4 matching squares

Select sets in this manner until you have 12 stacks of squares. I made a stack for each block, layering the squares of each print in order, starting with the center square. In general, I tried to use darker colors toward the center of the block and varied the look of the blocks by using contrasting colors in some blocks, while creating gradual shade changes in other blocks. Here's an example of a stack for one of my blocks (from the center out):

- 1 white center square
- 4 red solid squares
- 8 pink check squares
- 12 medium pink squares
- 12 white print squares
- 8 aqua floral squares
- 4 aqua check squares

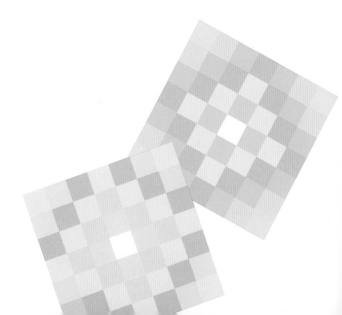

Designed and pieced by ALLISON JENSEN; quilted by STAR BEAR

Making the Blocks

Press seam allowances in the directions indicated by the arrows.

Using one stack of squares and one white square, lay out the squares in seven rows of seven squares each. Sew the squares into rows. Join the rows to make a block. Make 12 blocks measuring 14½" square, including seam allowances.

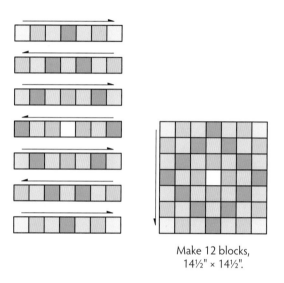

Make 12 blocks,
14½" × 14½".

Assembling the Quilt Top

1 Join four print 1½" squares and three white rectangles to make a sashing row. Make five rows measuring 1½" × 46½", including seam allowances.

Make 5 sashing rows,
1½" × 46½".

2 Join four white rectangles and three blocks to make a block row. Make four rows measuring 14½" × 46½", including seam allowances.

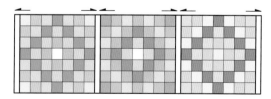

Make 4 block rows,
14½" × 46½".

3 Join the sashing and block rows as shown in the quilt assembly diagram. The quilt top should measure 46½" × 61½", including seam allowances.

4 Join the aqua 4½"-wide strips end to end. From the pieced strip, cut two 61½"-long strips and two 54½"-long strips. Sew the longer strips to opposite sides of the quilt center. Sew the shorter strips to the top and bottom edges to complete the quilt top. The quilt top should measure 54½" × 69½".

Finishing the Quilt

For more details on any finishing steps, visit ShopMartingale.com/HowtoQuilt for free downloadable information.

1 Layer the quilt top with batting and backing; baste the layers together.

2 Quilt by hand or machine. The quilt shown is machine quilted with an allover Baptist fan design.

3 Use the green 2½"-wide strips to make binding and then attach the binding to the quilt.

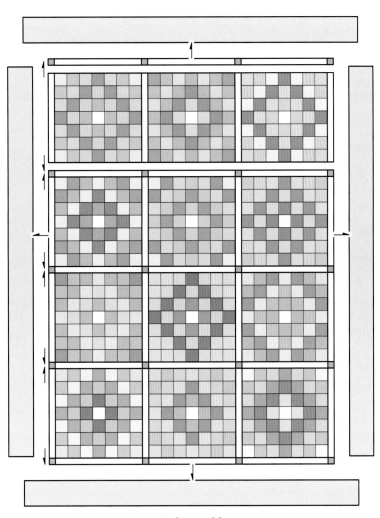

Quilt assembly

FABRICS USED

Handmade and Hello Darling
by Bonnie and Camille
for Moda Fabrics

Strawberry Jam
by Corey Yoder
for Moda Fabrics

Little Snippets
by Bonnie and Camille
for Moda Fabrics

Cozy at Home

If there's one thing I learned living in Russia for a year as a missionary, it's that rugs make everything cozier! Russians even hang large ones on the walls of their homes to add color, softness, and warmth. This is my take on the classic rag rug, using pressed strips for a more polished look. Use leftover binding strips or precut rolls, or if you prefer a scrappier rug, cut strips from yardage.

· ·

Materials

- 42 strips, 2½" × 42", of assorted prints for rug*
- Glue stick or glue pen
- White cotton thread

*If you'd like to make a 34"-diameter rug, you'll need 84 strips, 2½" × 42".

Making the Rug

1 Choose three strips. Trim 10" from one end of the first strip and trim 5" from one end of the second strip. Do not trim the third strip. This way, the joins will be staggered when you add more strips.

2 Fold each strip from step 1 in half lengthwise, wrong sides together, and press the fold. Unfold and turn the raw edges of the strip to the center crease; press. Refold on the center crease and steam press the strip to make a crisp edge. Repeat to press each of the remaining strips in the same way.

3 Stack the first three strips from step 2 on top of each other and stitch them together along the selvage end. Begin braiding the strips, making sure to fold and not twist the strips. Continue braiding until you reach the end of the shortest strip. Pin or use a clip to hold the strips in place. Press well for good measure.

4 At your sewing machine, tuck the beginning end under itself. Begin to stitch the braid into a coil using a wide zigzag stitch and cotton thread. Make sure to form the coil to the left of your presser foot so that as it grows, you have room for the rug. If you're facing the wrong way, turn the braid over. Place the edges of the braid side by side and sew a zigzag stitch directly between the two edges. The beginning will look and feel disastrous. Persist! Stitch where you can to form a circle. The process will get easier as you get past the center.

5 When you are about 12" from the end of the shortest strip, add a new strip, referring to "Adding a New Strip" on page 21. Continue stitching and adding new strips until the rug is the desired size.

Build It Up

If your sewing machine isn't inset into a sewing table, as your rug grows larger you'll need something like thick books, board games, or puzzle boxes to stack up around your machine to hold the rug level and flat, otherwise you'll end up with more of a bowl shape.

6 When you reach the end of the last braid, trim the strips so the ends are even. Tuck the ends under the end of the braid and stitch in place. Continue to zigzag stitch all the way around the outer edge of the rug to reinforce it. Then change to a straight stitch and sew through the center of each braid (see close-up photo on page 20), moving from the outermost edges inward. When the turns get too tight, backstitch to secure, and then stitch horizontal and vertical lines across the center, beginning and ending each line with backstitching. In the same way, stitch lines diagonally in both directions across the center.

7 If your rug isn't flat, you can spray it with water or starch. Then iron the rug or place heavy books around the edges overnight. The rug will eventually comply with its flat destiny!

ADDING A NEW STRIP

When you reach the end of each strip, you'll need to add another strip.

1 Dab glue on the inside edges at the end of the shortest strip of the braid.

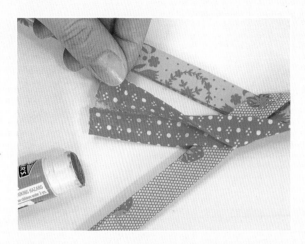

2 Place the new strip inside the first strip. Press the braid and stitch the braid to the coil. Continue braiding until you reach the end of the next shortest strip.

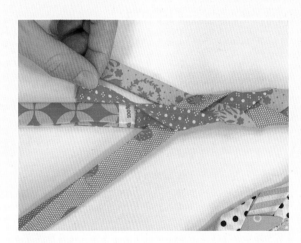

Peppermint Party

Most people either love mint or hate it, and I'm definitely a mint lover! It was a delight to dream up these strings of candies in shades of cinnamon, spearmint, peppermint, and sweet mint. The contrast with the dark background fabric really makes the candy pop. If you're not a mint lover, use bright summery prints and a cool blue background and call your blocks beach balls or umbrellas.

• •

Materials

Yardage is based on 42"-wide fabric.

- 42 *pairs* of squares, 5" × 5", of assorted prints for blocks (84 total)
- 1¾ yards of white solid for blocks*
- 3 yards of black solid for background
- ⅝ yard of red diagonal stripe for binding
- 3¾ yards of fabric for backing
- 67" × 77" piece of batting

You can use 84 precut squares, 5" × 5", instead of the yardage listed.

Cutting

All measurements include ¼" seam allowances.

From the white solid, cut:
11 strips, 5" × 42"; crosscut into 84 squares, 5" × 5"

From the black solid, cut:
25 strips, 2½" × 42"; crosscut into:
    42 rectangles, 2½" × 10½"
    42 rectangles, 2½" × 8½"
12 strips, 2¾" × 42"; crosscut into 168 squares, 2¾" × 2¾"

From the red stripe, cut:
7 strips, 2½" × 42"

Making the Blocks

Press seam allowances in the directions indicated by the arrows.

1 Draw a diagonal line from corner to corner on the wrong side of the white squares. Layer a marked square on a print 5" square, right sides together. Sew ¼" from both sides of the drawn line. Cut the unit apart on the marked line to make two half-square-triangle units. Trim the units to measure 4½" square, including seam allowances. Make 42 sets of four matching units (168 total).

Make 42 sets of 4 matching units.

2 Lay out four matching half-square-triangle units in two rows of two, noting the orientation of the units. Sew the units into rows. Join the rows to make a pinwheel unit. Make 42 units measuring 8½" square, including seam allowances.

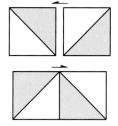 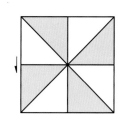

Make 42 units, 8½" × 8½".

3 Draw a diagonal line from corner to corner on the wrong side of the black squares. Place a marked square on each corner of a pinwheel unit. Sew on the marked lines. Trim the excess corner fabric, ¼" from the stitched lines. Make 42 candy units measuring 8½" square, including seam allowances.

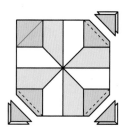 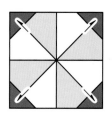

Make 42 units, 8½" × 8½".

Designed by ALLISON JENSEN; pieced by LAUREL HORCHEM;
quilted by EMILEE HATHAWAY

4 Sew a black 2½" × 8½" rectangle to the left edge of a candy unit. Sew a black 2½" × 10½" rectangle to the top edge to make a block. Make 42 blocks measuring 10½" square, including seam allowances.

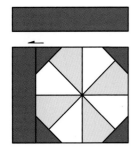
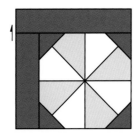

Make 42 blocks,
10½" × 10½".

Assembling the Quilt Top

Lay out the blocks in seven rows of six blocks each, rotating every other block as shown in the quilt assembly diagram. Sew the blocks into rows. Join the rows to make a quilt top measuring 60½" × 70½".

Finishing the Quilt

For more details on any finishing steps, visit ShopMartingale.com/HowtoQuilt for free downloadable information.

1 Layer the quilt top with batting and backing; baste the layers together.

2 Quilt by hand or machine. The quilt shown is machine quilted with an allover design of diagonal squares.

3 Use the red stripe 2½"-wide strips to make binding and then attach the binding to the quilt.

Quilt assembly

North Star

Have you ever wanted to sew a quilt big enough for your bed but felt intimidated by the size? This pattern provides big impact with minimal sewing time, thanks to one big block and wide borders. Add some big-stitch hand quilting to your Star block and you've got a masterpiece.

FINISHED QUILT
88½" × 88½"

FINISHED BLOCK
40" × 40"

Materials

Yardage is based on 42"-wide fabric.

- 1⅞ yards of navy solid for block and binding
- 3⅜ yards of white solid for block and inner border
- 3⅝ yards of navy gingham for block and outer border
- 8⅛ yards of fabric for backing
- 97" × 97" piece of batting
- Aqua embroidery floss for big-stitch quilting

FABRICS USED

Kona Cotton in Windsor
by Robert Kaufman Fabrics

1" Gingham Check in Navy
by Riley Blake Designs

Confetti Cotton in Riley White
by Riley Blake Designs

Cutting

All measurements include ¼" seam allowances.

From the navy solid, cut:

2 strips, 6" × 42"; crosscut into 8 squares, 6" × 6"

4 strips, 5½" × 42"; crosscut into 24 squares,
   5½" × 5½"

10 strips, 2½" × 42"

From the white solid, cut:

6 strips, 12½" × 42"

1 strip, 10½" × 42"; crosscut into:

   1 square, 10½" × 10½"

   4 rectangles, 5½" × 10½"

2 strips, 6" × 42"; crosscut into 8 squares, 6" × 6"

2 strips, 5½" × 42"; crosscut into 4 rectangles,
   5½" × 15½"

From the navy gingham, cut:

8 strips, 12½" × 42"

3 strips, 5½" × 42"; crosscut into:

   8 rectangles, 5½" × 10½"

   4 squares, 5½" × 5½"

Making the Block

Press seam allowances in the directions indicated
by the arrows.

1   Draw a diagonal line from corner to corner
on the wrong side of 20 navy solid 5½"
squares. Place marked squares on opposite corners
of the white 10½" square, right sides together. Sew
on the marked line. Trim the excess corner fabric, ¼"
from the stitched line. Place marked squares on the
remaining corners of the square. Sew and trim as
before to make a center unit measuring 10½" square,
including seam allowances.

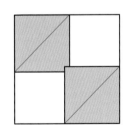
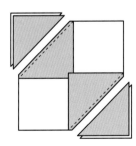

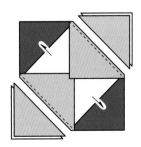

Make 1 unit,
10½" × 10½".

2 Place a marked navy square on one end of a gingham rectangle, right sides together and noting the direction of the marked line. Sew on the marked line. Trim the excess corner fabric, ¼" from the stitched line. Place a marked square on the other end of the rectangle, noting the direction of the marked line. Sew and trim as before to make a unit. Make four units measuring 5½" × 10½", including seam allowances. Reverse the placement of the navy squares to make four reversed units.

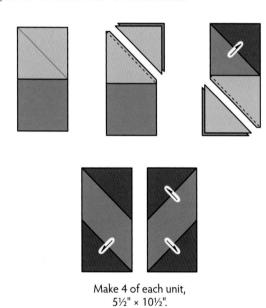

Make 4 of each unit,
5½" × 10½".

3 Join the units from step 2 in pairs to make an A unit. Make four units measuring 10½" square, including seam allowances.

Make 4 units,
10½" × 10½".

4 Draw a diagonal line from corner to corner on the wrong side of the white 6" squares. Layer a marked square on a navy solid 6" square, right sides together. Sew ¼" from both sides of the drawn line. Cut the unit apart on the marked line to make two half-square-triangle units. Trim the units to measure 5½" square, including seam allowances. Make 16 units.

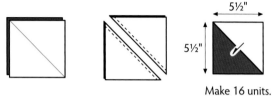

Make 16 units.

5 Join two half-square-triangle units, noting the orientation of the units, to make a B unit. Make four units measuring 5½" × 10½", including seam allowances.

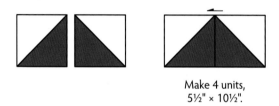

Make 4 units,
5½" × 10½".

6 Sew a B unit to the top of an A unit to make a side unit. Make four units measuring 10½" × 15½", including seam allowances.

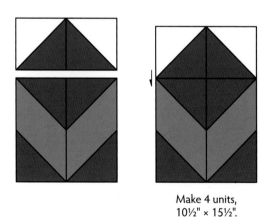

Make 4 units,
10½" × 15½".

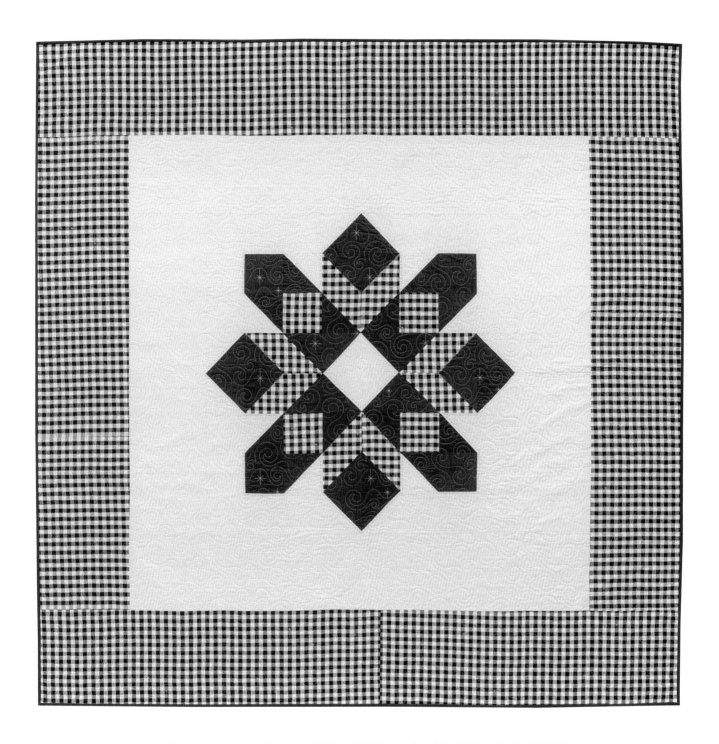

Designed and pieced by ALLISON JENSEN; quilted by SHELLEY CANTRELL

Reverse Colorway

The pattern looks wonderful if you reverse the navy and white colors. The quilt looks like a snowflake!

7 Lay out two half-square-triangle units, one navy 5½" square, and one gingham square in two rows of two. Join the pieces to make a four-patch unit. Make four units measuring 10½" square, including seam allowances.

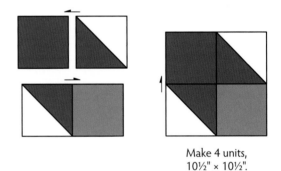

Make 4 units,
10½" × 10½".

8 Sew a white 5½" × 10½" rectangle to the left edge of a four-patch unit from step 7, noting the orientation of the unit. Sew a white 5½" × 15½" rectangle to the top of the unit to make a corner unit. Make four units measuring 15½" square, including seam allowances.

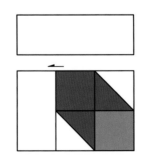
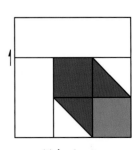

Make 4 units,
15½" × 15½".

9 Lay out the corner units, side units, and center unit in three rows of three, noting the orientation of the units. Sew the units into rows. Join the rows to make a block measuring 40½" square, including seam allowances.

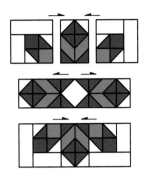

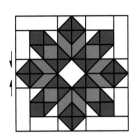

Make 1 block, 40½" × 40½".

Assembling the Quilt Top

1 Join the white 12½"-wide strips end to end. From the pieced strip, cut two 64½"-long strips and two 40½"-long strips. Sew the shorter strips to opposite sides of the block. Sew the longer strips to the top and bottom edges. The quilt top should measure 64½" square, including seam allowances.

2 Join the gingham 12½"-wide strips end to end using a straight seam and aligning the checks in the fabric. From the pieced strip, cut two 88½"-long strips and two 64½"-long strips. Sew the shorter strips to opposite sides of the quilt top. Sew the longer strips to the top and bottom edges. The quilt top should measure 88½" square.

Finishing the Quilt

For more details on any finishing steps, visit ShopMartingale.com/HowtoQuilt for free downloadable information.

1 Layer the quilt top with batting and backing; baste the layers together.

2 Quilt by hand or machine. The quilt shown is machine quilted with an allover swirl and star design. After machine quilting, use aqua embroidery floss to sew a running stitch around the perimeter of the center star design, ¼" beyond the seamlines.

3 Use the navy solid 2½"-wide strips to make binding and then attach the binding to the quilt.

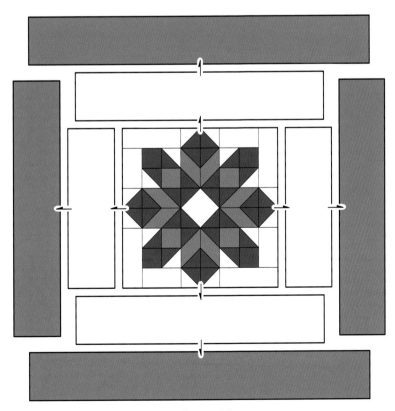

Quilt assembly

FABRICS USED

Kona Cotton in Snow
by Robert Kaufman Fabrics

Simple Gifts

Show off your favorite Christmas fabrics with a sweet holiday runner using 10" precut squares or fabrics from your stash. The table runner makes a quick gift—for someone else or for yourself!

. . . .

Materials

Yardage is based on 42"-wide fabric.

- 5 squares, 10" × 10", of assorted prints for ribbons and bows (A)
- 5 squares, 10" × 10", of assorted complementary prints for wrapping paper (B)
- ⅜ yard of white solid for sashing and border
- ⅜ yard of green diagonal stripe for binding
- 1 yard of fabric for backing
- 19" × 62" piece of batting

Cutting

All measurements include ¼" seam allowances. Refer to the cutting diagrams on page 36 as needed to cut the A and B squares.

From *each* of the A squares, cut:
1 rectangle, 1½" × 9½" (5 total)
2 rectangles, 1½" × 4½" (10 total)
4 squares, 2½" × 2½" (20 total)

From *each* of the B squares, cut:
8 rectangles, 2½" × 4½" (40 total)

From the white solid, cut:
5 strips, 2¼" × 42"; crosscut *2 of the strips* into:
    4 strips, 2¼" × 9½"
    2 strips, 2¼" × 13"

Continued on page 36

Making the Blocks

Press seam allowances in the directions indicated by the arrows.

1 Draw a diagonal line from corner to corner on the wrong side of four matching A squares. Place a marked square on one end of a B rectangle, right sides together. Sew on the marked line. Trim the excess corner fabric, ¼" from the stitched line. Make four matching units measuring 2½" × 4½", including seam allowances.

Make 4 units,
2½" × 4½".

2 Sew a matching B rectangle to the top edge of a unit to make a corner unit. Make four units measuring 4½" square, including seam allowances.

Make 4 units,
4½" × 4½".

3 Lay out four corner units, two A 1½" × 4½" rectangles, and one A 1½" × 9½" rectangle in three rows. The A rectangles should match the triangles in the corner units. Sew the pieces into rows. Join the rows to make a block measuring 9½" square, including seam allowances. Repeat the steps to make a total of five blocks.

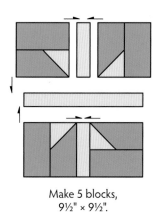

Make 5 blocks,
9½" × 9½".

Continued from page 35

From the green stripe, cut:

4 strips, 2½" × 42"

```
          10"
┌──────────────────────────┐
│      1½" × 9½"            │
├────────────┬─────────────┤
│ 1½" × 4½"  │  1½" × 4½"   │
├─────┬─────┬──────┬───────┤
│2½"  │2½"  │2½"   │2½"     │
│ ×   │ ×   │ ×    │ ×      │ 10"
│2½"  │2½"  │2½"   │2½"     │
├─────┴─────┴──────┴───────┤
│                          │
│                          │
└──────────────────────────┘
```

Cutting for A squares

```
          10"
┌─────────────┬─────────────┐
│ 2½" × 4½"   │  2½" × 4½"   │
├─────────────┼─────────────┤
│ 2½" × 4½"   │  2½" × 4½"   │
├─────────────┼─────────────┤ 10"
│ 2½" × 4½"   │  2½" × 4½"   │
├─────────────┼─────────────┤
│ 2½" × 4½"   │  2½" × 4½"   │
└─────────────┴─────────────┘
```

Cutting for B squares

Designed and pieced by ALLISON JENSEN; quilted by STARLIT BEAR

Assembling the Table-Runner Top

1 Lay out the blocks and white 2¼" × 9½" strips, placing a white strip between each of the blocks. Join the blocks and strips to make a table-runner center measuring 9½" × 52½", including seam allowances.

2 Join the three remaining white 2¼" × 42" strips end to end. From the pieced strip, cut two 52½"-long strips. Sew the strips to the long edges of the table-runner center. Sew the white 2¼" × 13" strips to the short ends of the table runner. The table runner should measure 56" × 13".

Finishing the Table Runner

For more details on any finishing steps, visit ShopMartingale.com/HowtoQuilt for free downloadable information.

1 Layer the table-runner top with batting and backing; baste the layers together.

2 Quilt by hand or machine. The table runner shown is machine quilted with straight lines, swirls, and feathers in the blocks. You can quilt the same designs in each block or use a combination of different designs as in the table runner shown. A continuous feather design is quilted in the border.

3 Use the green stripe 2½"-wide strips to make binding and then attach the binding to the table runner.

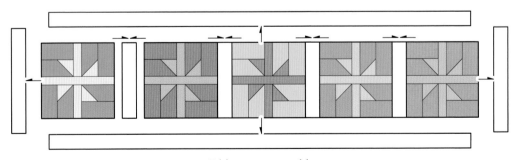

Table-runner assembly

Soothing & Serene

In a neutral room setting, add a pop of color and comfort with a throw that makes an inviting spot for a respite. English paper-piecing techniques are used to construct the stars in each block, which makes this a great take-along project.

FINISHED QUILT
60½" × 72½"

FINISHED BLOCK
12" × 12"

FABRICS USED

Kona Cotton in Snow
by Robert Kaufman Fabrics

Handmade
by Bonnie and Camille
for Moda Fabrics

Materials

Yardage is based on 42"-wide fabric. Fat eighths measure 9" × 21".

- 30 fat eighths of assorted prints in green, aqua, and pink for blocks
- 1⅜ yards of red print for blocks
- 5⅜ yards of white solid for blocks
- ⅝ yard of aqua print for binding
- 3¾ yards of fabric for backing
- 67" × 79" piece of batting
- Cardstock *OR* 2 precut templates (2½" eight-point diamond and 2½" square)
- Water-soluble glue pen (optional)

Cutting

All measurements include ¼" seam allowances.

From *each* of the assorted prints, cut:
8 squares, 3¼" × 3¼" (240 total)

From the red solid, cut:
18 strips, 2½" × 42"; crosscut into 120 rectangles, 2½" × 5"

From the white solid, cut:
10 strips, 13" × 42"; crosscut into 30 squares, 13" × 13"
18 strips, 2½" × 42"; crosscut into 120 rectangles, 2½" × 5"

From the aqua print, cut:
7 strips, 2½" × 42"

Preparing the Pieces

1 Use the patterns on page 43 to photocopy the diamond and square onto cardstock. Make 240 copies of each. Cut out each template on the marked line. If you're using precut templates, you can skip this step.

2 Pin or glue a diamond template to the wrong side of each red and white rectangle. Cut out each fabric shape, adding ⅜" seam allowance all around the paper template. Fold the seam allowance over the edge of the template. Use a needle and thread to hand baste the seam allowances to the template, stitching through all the layers and making sharp folds at each corner. The folding will create tails; leave the tails hanging out as shown. Make 120 red diamonds and 120 white diamonds.

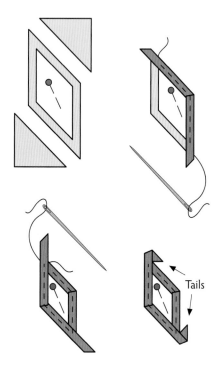

3 Pin or glue a square template to the wrong side of each print 3¼" square. Repeat step 2 to baste the seam allowances to the template. Make 30 sets of eight matching squares (240 total).

Making the Blocks

1 Thread a needle with a single strand of thread and tie a knot in the end.

2 Place one red and one white diamond right sides together. Whipstitch them together from corner to corner, catching only the folded edges. Do not stitch through the paper.

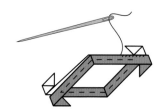
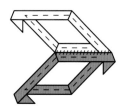

3 Repeat step 2 to join four red and four white diamonds, alternating colors to make an eight-pointed star. Make 30 stars.

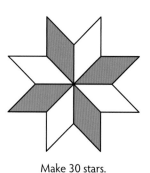

Make 30 stars.

Designed by ALLISON JENSEN; pieced by JEANIE MAHER; quilted by AMANDA RUCKER

4 Sew matching squares between the star points to complete a star unit. Remove all of the basting stitches and paper templates and press well. Make 30 units.

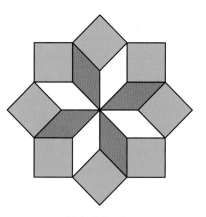

Make 30 units.

5 Fold a white 13" square in half vertically and horizontally. Center a paper-pieced unit on the white square, aligning the points on the block with the fold lines. Pin or glue baste in place. Topstitch around the perimeter of the unit, stitching ⅛" from the folded outer edge. Trim the block to measure 12½" square, including seam allowances. Make 30 blocks.

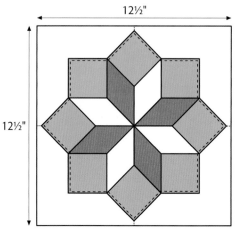

12½"

12½"

Make 30 blocks.

Assembling the Quilt Top

Lay out the blocks in six rows of five blocks each. Sew the blocks into rows. Join the rows. Press seam allowances in the directions indicated by the arrows. The quilt top should measure 60½" × 72½".

Finishing the Quilt

For more details on any finishing steps, visit ShopMartingale.com/HowtoQuilt for free downloadable information.

1. Layer the quilt top with batting and backing; baste the layers together.

2. Quilt by hand or machine. The quilt shown is machine quilted with an allover clamshell design.

3. Use the aqua 2½"-wide strips to make binding and then attach the binding to the quilt.

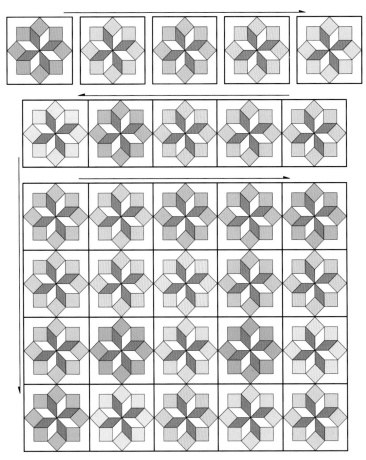

Quilt assembly

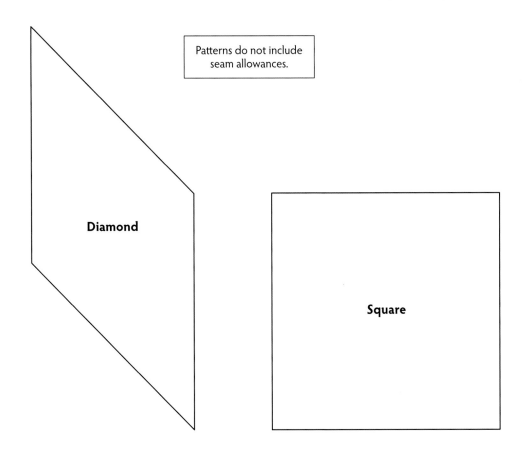

Patterns do not include seam allowances.

Diamond

Square

FINISHED QUILT

60½" × 72½"

FINISHED BLOCK

12" × 12"

FABRICS USED

Kona Cotton in Bone
and Cardinal
by Robert Kaufman Fabrics

Le Creme Swiss Dot in Gray
by Riley Blake Designs

Swell Christmas Santa
by Urban Chiks for
Moda Fabrics

Red Rover

I have always adored the color red. In Russian, the words for *red*, *painted*, and *beautiful* are all almost exactly the same. I couldn't agree more! I love to mix prints and solids in quilts; here I used a bold red solid next to softer creams and low-volume prints. Red rover, red rover, send more reds right over!

• •

Materials

Yardage is based on 42"-wide fabric. Fat eighths measure 9" × 21". Fat quarters measure 18" × 21".

- ⅞ yard of red solid for blocks
- ⅞ yard of cream dot for blocks
- 1¼ yards of cream solid for blocks
- 30 fat eighths *OR* 15 fat quarters of low-volume prints in pink, green, gray, and cream for blocks (referred to collectively as "light")
- ⅝ yard of gray stripe for binding
- 3¾ yards of fabric for backing
- 67" × 79" piece of batting

Cutting

All measurements include ¼" seam allowances.

From the red solid, cut:
13 strips, 2" × 42"

From the cream dot, cut:
13 strips, 2" × 42"

From the cream solid, cut:
11 strips, 3½" × 42"; crosscut into 120 squares, 3½" × 3½"

From the light prints, cut a *total* of:
240 squares, 3½" × 3½"

From the gray stripe, cut:
7 strips, 2½" × 42"

Making the Blocks

Press seam allowances in the directions indicated by the arrows.

1 Join red and cream dot strips along one long edge to make a strip set. Make 13 strip sets measuring 3½" × 42", including seam allowances. Crosscut the strip sets into 240 segments, 2" × 3½".

Make 13 strip sets, 3½" × 42".
Cut 240 segments, 2" × 3½".

2 Join two segments from step 1 to make a four-patch unit. Make 120 units measuring 3½" square, including seam allowances.

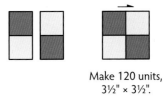

Make 120 units,
3½" × 3½".

3 Lay out two four-patch units and two different light squares in two rows of two. Sew the pieces into rows. Join the rows to make an A unit. Make 60 units measuring 6½" square, including seam allowances.

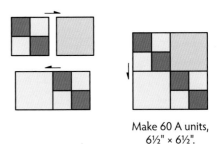

Make 60 A units,
6½" × 6½".

Designed and quilted by ALLISON JENSEN; pieced by SHELLEY CANTRELL

Assembling the Quilt Top

Lay out the blocks in six rows of five blocks each as shown. Sew the blocks into rows. Join the rows to make a quilt top measuring 60½" × 72½".

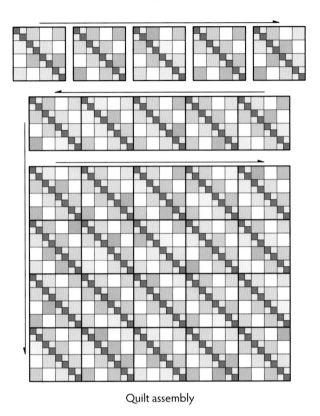

Quilt assembly

4 Lay out two cream solid squares and two different light squares in two rows of two. Sew the squares into rows. Join the rows to make a B unit. Make 60 units measuring 6½" square, including seam allowances.

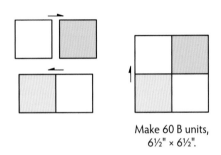

Make 60 B units,
6½" × 6½".

5 Lay out two A units and two B units in two rows, noting the orientation of the red squares. Sew the units into rows. Join the rows to make a block. Make 30 blocks measuring 12½" square, including seam allowances.

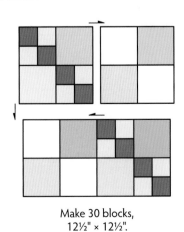

Make 30 blocks,
12½" × 12½".

Finishing the Quilt

For more details on any finishing steps, visit ShopMartingale.com/HowtoQuilt for free downloadable information.

1 Layer the quilt top with batting and backing; baste the layers together.

2 Quilt by hand or machine. The quilt shown is machine quilted with straight and wavy lines that are alternately stitched diagonally through the squares.

3 Use the gray stripe 2½"-wide strips to make binding and then attach the binding to the quilt.

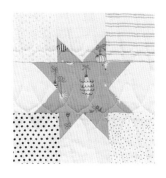

Star Light, Star Bright

A field of colorful stars twinkling atop a light color background has an unexpected feel that I find magical. Patches of texture, sparkle, text prints, fussy cuts, and a sassy pop of aqua binding, all in a very modern color palette, makes for a quilt full of surprises and discoveries. This is a wonderful scrap buster for low-volume and star prints alike, and could be made to suit any season.

FINISHED QUILT
60" × 75"

FINISHED BLOCK
7½" × 7½"

FABRICS USED

Kona Cotton in Snow
by Robert Kaufman Fabrics

Vintage Holiday
by Bonnie and Camille
for Moda Fabrics
(border)

Materials

Yardage is based on 42"-wide fabric. Fat quarters measure 18" × 21".

- 10 fat quarters of assorted light prints for blocks
- 16 squares, 10" × 10", of assorted solids and prints for blocks (referred to collectively as "dark")
- 2 yards of white solid for blocks
- ⅞ yard of white print for border
- ⅝ yard of black diagonal stripe for binding
- 4½ yards of fabric for backing
- 66" × 81" piece of batting

Cutting

All measurements include ¼" seam allowances.

From *each* of the assorted light prints, cut

25 squares, 3" × 3" (250 total)

From *1* of the light prints, cut:

2 squares, 3" × 3" (you'll now have 252 squares total)

From *each* of the assorted dark prints, cut:

2 squares, 3" × 3" (32 total; 1 is extra)

16 squares, 1¾" × 1¾" (256 total; 8 are extra)

From the white solid, cut:

22 strips, 3" × 42"; crosscut into 284 squares, 3" × 3"

From the white print, cut:

7 strips, 4" × 42"

From the black stripe, cut:

8 strips, 2½" × 42"

Making the Nine Patch Blocks

Press seam allowances in the directions indicated by the arrows.

Lay out five white and four light 3" squares in three rows of three squares each. Sew the squares into rows. Join the rows to make a Nine Patch block. Make 32 blocks measuring 8" square, including the seam allowances.

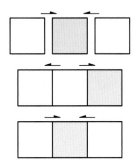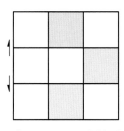

Make 32 Nine Patch blocks, 8" × 8".

Making the Star Blocks

1 Draw a diagonal line from corner to corner on the wrong side of the dark 1¾" squares. Place a marked square on one corner of a white square, right sides together. Sew on the marked line. Trim the excess corner fabric, ¼" from the stitched line. Place a marked square on an adjacent corner of the square. Sew and trim as before to make a star-point unit measuring 3" square, including seam allowances. Make 31 sets of four matching units (124 total).

Make 31 sets of four matching units, 3" × 3".

2 Lay out four different light squares, four matching star-point units, and one dark 3" square in three rows of three. The dark square should match the triangles in the star-point units. Sew the pieces into rows. Join the rows to make a Star block. Make 31 blocks measuring 8" square, including seam allowances.

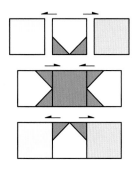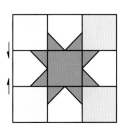

Make 31 Star blocks, 8" × 8".

Designed and pieced by ALLISON JENSEN; quilted by EMILEE HATHAWAY

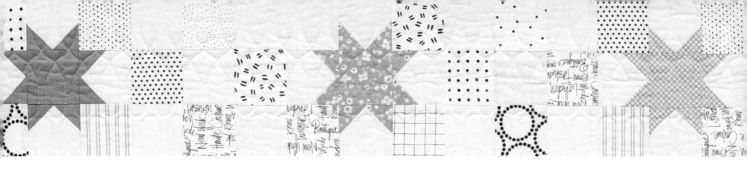

Assembling the Quilt Top

1 Lay out the blocks in nine rows of seven blocks each, alternating the blocks in each row and from row to row as shown in the quilt assembly diagram below. Sew the blocks into rows. Join the rows to make a quilt center measuring 53" × 68", including seam allowances.

2 Join the white print 4"-wide strips end to end. From the pieced strip, cut two 68"-long strips and two 60"-long strips. Sew the longer strips to opposite sides of the quilt center. Sew the shorter strips to the top and bottom edges. The quilt top should measure 60" × 75".

Finishing the Quilt

For more details on any finishing steps, visit ShopMartingale.com/HowtoQuilt for free downloadable information.

1 Layer the quilt top with batting and backing; baste the layers together.

2 Quilt by hand or machine. The quilt shown is machine quilted with an allover design of horizontal rows of loops.

3 Use the black stripe 2½"-wide strips to make binding and then attach the binding to the quilt.

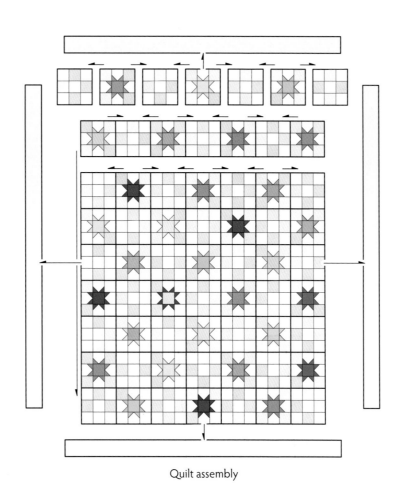

Quilt assembly

FABRICS USED

Kona Cotton in Ice Frappe, Poppy, and Grass Green
by Robert Kaufman Fabrics (pillow backs)

Happy Scrappy Pillows

One-color scrap projects are some of my favorite things to sew. They don't require much thought or planning—just grab your scraps and start cutting any print you can find in that color. In this case, the squares are cut 2½", so these pillows are perfect for lonely leftover precuts too. The beauty of these projects lies in the wide range of tones and hues within each color group.

Materials

- 81 squares, 2½" × 2½", of assorted single-color prints for pillow front
- 1 square, 20" × 20", of coordinating print for pillow back
- 2 rectangles, 1" × 5", of coordinating print for zipper
- 2 squares, 20" × 20", of batting
- 20" × 20" pillow form or insert
- 16"-long nylon zipper to match pillow front

Making the Pillow Front and Back

Press seam allowances in the directions indicated by the arrows.

1 Lay out the print squares in nine rows of nine squares each. Sew the squares into rows. Join the rows to make a pillow top measuring 18½" square, including seam allowances.

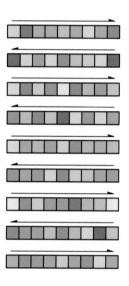

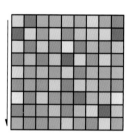

Make 1 pillow top,
18½" × 18½".

The Value of Scraps

When planning scrap placement, keep in mind the value of each fabric, or how dark or light it is. If you aren't sure, snap a photo of your layout in black and white (phone cameras have this option) and you'll see that different fabrics can range in appearance from nearly black to white. Try to spread the squares out evenly, and not have any two squares with the same value touching. This will make your project more pleasing to the eye.

2 Layer the pillow front with batting; baste the layers together. Quilt by hand or machine. The pillow shown is machine quilted with evenly spaced lines using a decorative stitch (or you can quilt straight lines). You could also stitch lines diagonally from corner to corner or stitch lines from side to side.

3 Layer the pillow back with batting; baste. Quilt by hand or machine as described in step 2.

4 Trim the pillow front and back to measure 18½" square, including seam allowances.

Finishing the Pillow

1 Fold each 1" × 5" rectangle in half crosswise, wrong sides together. Place the folded edges of the rectangles next to the stops at each end of the zipper. Open the zipper if needed so you don't sew over the zipper pull. Edgestitch along the fold two or three times. Trim the zipper to measure 18½" long.

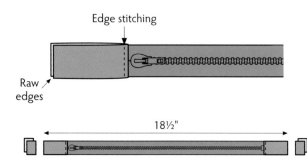

2 Place the zipper along one edge of the pillow front, right sides together. Sew along the edge of the zipper, about ⅛" from the teeth. I use a walking foot, but you can also use a zipper foot. When you get to the zipper pull, stop with the needle in the down position, lift the presser foot, and carefully slide the pull behind the presser foot. Then lower the presser foot and continue sewing to the end.

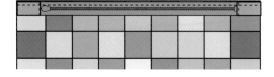

Decorating with Pillows

I love having a couch covered in handmade pillows, especially those that are holiday specific. Simple designs like this are versatile for holiday use. Put a green pillow out in March for St. Patrick's Day and to celebrate spring. A red pillow can stay out after Christmas through Valentine's Day. Make one in every color of the rainbow and you'll have any season or holiday covered, with lots of fun combinations too!

ACHIEVING PERFECT PILLOW FLUFFINESS

- The finished size of the pillow cover should be about 10% smaller than the size of the pillow form or insert. For example, if your pillow form states that it's 20" square, make your cover about 18" square. This prevents sad, saggy pillows.

- Using a zipper instead of an envelope backing will ensure that the pillow keeps its perky shape for years to come.

- Use batting under the fabric on both the pillow front and back. It can be quilted on, or even just spray basted. This will give your pillow cover body and help it last longer.

- For the best weight and feel, use down pillow forms or inserts. Polyester tends to get lumpy and flat over time. You can find inexpensive down pillow forms at IKEA worldwide stores or search online for IKEA Fjadrar. I usually use the 20" square insert, but I have also used their lumbar pillow as well as the larger square size.

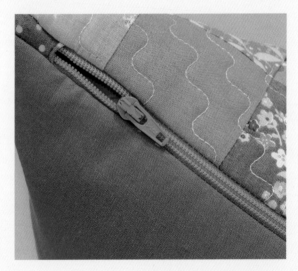

3 Repeat step 2 to sew the pillow back to the opposite side of the zipper.

4 Make sure the zipper is unzipped halfway. You will be turning the pillow inside out through the open zipper, so you don't want to forget this step.

5 Place the pillow front and back right sides together. Fold the rectangles at the ends of the zipper inward and flatten.

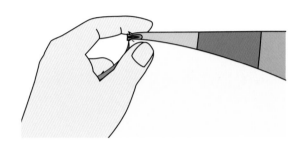

6 Using a ¼" seam allowance, sew around the remaining three edges of the pillow, starting and ending with a backstitch. Backstitch at each corner to reinforce the seams. Sew around the three sides again to reinforce the seams. Trim the corners. Turn the pillow right side out, pushing out the corners. Press well.

7 Unzip the pillow. Insert the pillow form and close the zipper.

Holiday Charm

Get your precuts ready! I had fun mixing up the new Urban Chiks Christmas line with some of their older prints. The straight-line quilting enhances the piecing design, resulting in a simple, classic quilt.

· ·

FINISHED QUILT
60½" × 76½"

FINISHED BLOCK
4" × 8"

FABRICS USED

Kona Cotton in Snow
by Robert Kaufman Fabrics

Sweet Christmas
and other lines
by Urban Chiks for
Moda Fabrics

Materials

Yardage is based on 42"-wide fabric.

- 143 squares, 5" × 5", of medium and dark prints (referred to collectively as "dark") for half-square-triangle units*
- 3¼ yards of white solid for half-square-triangle units**
- ⅝ yard of green dot for binding
- 4⅝ yards of fabric for backing
- 67" × 83" piece of batting

Purchase 4 packs of precut 5"×5" squares OR purchase 1 pack of precut 10"×10" squares and cut 36 of the squares in half vertically and horizontally to yield 144 squares, 5"×5" (1 is extra).

**You can use 143 precut squares, 5"×5", instead of the yardage listed.*

Cutting

All measurements include ¼" seam allowances.

From the white solid, cut:
21 strips, 5" × 42"; crosscut into 143 squares, 5" × 5"

From the green dot, cut:
8 strips, 2½" × 42"

Making the Blocks

Press seam allowances in the directions indicated by the arrows.

1 Draw a diagonal line from corner to corner on the wrong side of each white square. Layer a marked square on a print square, right sides together. Sew ¼" from both sides of the drawn line. Cut the unit apart on the marked line to make two half-square-triangle units. Trim the units to measure 4½" square, including seam allowances. Make 286 units.

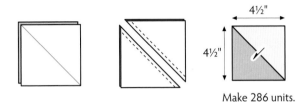

Make 286 units.

2 Join two matching half-square-triangle units, noting the orientation of the units, to make an A block. Make 72 blocks measuring 4½" × 8½", including seam allowances.

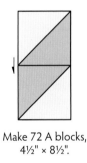

Make 72 A blocks,
4½" × 8½".

3 Repeat step 2 to make 63 B blocks, noting the orientation of the half-square-triangle units. The blocks should measure 4½" × 8½", including seam allowances. Set aside the remaining 16 half-square-triangle units.

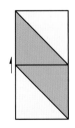

Make 63 B blocks,
4½" × 8½".

Assembling the Quilt Top

1 Join nine A blocks and one of the remaining half-square-triangle units to make an A column measuring 4½" × 76½", including seam allowances. Make eight A columns.

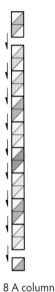

Make 8 A columns,
4½" × 76½".

2 Join nine B blocks and one half-square-triangle unit to make a B column. The column should measure 4½" × 76½", including seam allowances. Make seven B columns. You'll have one half-square-triangle unit left over for another project.

Make 7 B columns,
4½" × 76½".

Designed, pieced, and quilted by ALLISON JENSEN

3 Join the A and B columns, alternating them as shown. The quilt top should measure 60½" × 76½".

Quilt assembly

Finishing the Quilt

For more details on any finishing steps, visit ShopMartingale.com/HowtoQuilt for free downloadable information.

1 Layer the quilt top with batting and backing; baste the layers together.

2 Quilt by hand or machine. The quilt shown is machine quilted with evenly spaced vertical lines across the quilt top.

3 Use the green dot 2½"-wide strips to make binding and then attach the binding to the quilt.

About the Author

Allison Jensen is a lifelong creative and Californian. She dabbles in all kinds of artistic endeavors but loves quilting most of all. She learned to quilt in 2013 through library books and trial and error. Since then, she's made hundreds of quilts and loves it more all the time!

In 2016 she started her quilt-pattern business, Woodberry Way, named after the street in London where her mother grew up. Allison designs quilt patterns that are traditionally pieced and feature classic, orderly blocks. Her work has been published in various magazines including *McCall's Quilting, American Patchwork & Quilting, Love Patchwork & Quilting*, and *Modern Patchwork*. She particularly loves choosing fabrics for quiltmaking, combining prints from different designers and manufacturers into delightful color combinations. Allison's inspiration comes from traveling to new places, the beauty of nature, and her childhood.

Allison lives in Northern California with her husband and four young sons. Although she enjoys being a "boy mom," she appreciates that quilting gives her a place to enjoy all things floral and feminine. You can often find Allison chatting about Woodberry Way's current projects on Instagram (@woodberry_way) and sharing finished items on her blog (WoodberryWay.com).